The Beginner's Guide to Wine

BY JASON M. ARNOLD

EDITED BY WESLEY A. UPCHURCH

The Beginners Guide to Wine

ISBN: 9798656198578

TABLE OF CONTENTS

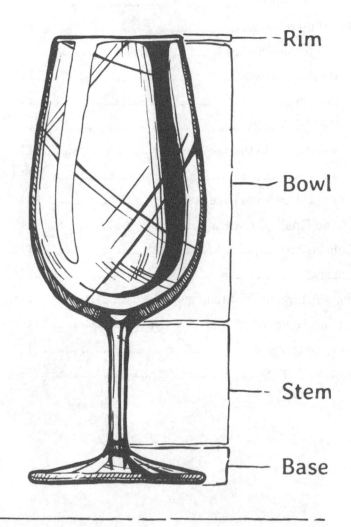

~Rim

Bowl

Stem

Base

The Anatomy of a Wine Glass

AN INTRODUCTION

"Wine is a passport to the world."

Thom Elkjer

Let's say you're in a wine store trying to find that perfect wine to serve at your evening get together. Before you ever walked into the store, you had an idea of what kind of wine you wanted. But now that you've arrived, you see the vast selection and feel a bit overwhelmed.

There are so many wines at so many different prices. You pick up a bottle that looks promising and buy it. You then hope that your dinner guests will be impressed. But how can you be sure? Don't worry, this is a common situation for someone just beginning in wine. But it doesn't have to be that way. Actually, with so many choices you should be able to find something that suits the occasion and not simply make a guess.

My goal is that by the time you finish this book, you'll be able to choose a bottle with confidence or even discuss wine with a wine steward without second guessing yourself. We'll start with the basics and build upon that foundation.

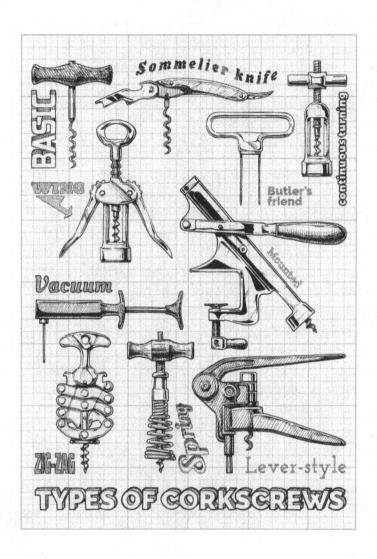

CHAPTER 1: THE BASICS OF WINE

"Wine is bottled poetry."

— Erin Morgenstern, The Night Circus

Before you can decide what wine to pair with a particular food or what wines to try when you attend a tasting, you really need to understand some of the basics of the subject. You should understand and be able to articulate what wine is. You will also do well understand the basic winemaking process. This includes understanding the major varieties of grapes used in winemaking.

The Basics of Wine also includes comprehension of the major types of wine. This process involves understanding the various approaches to defining or classifying wine. They range from color to taste. This chapter will begin at the beginning with a definition of wine, dive into its history, and then discuss how it's made.

WHAT IS WINE?

The simplest way to define wine is this. Wine is the fermented juice of wine grapes. Fermentation occurs when the sugar present in grape juice becomes, through the actions of yeast, alcohol. This is a totally natural process. The end result is that the grape juice becomes wine.

It's important to note that, fermentation can and does occur naturally, even without human intervention. But the human hand can help to produce a much more palatable and enjoyable product. While, the weight of grapes in a barrel can crush the fruit into juice, ferment and create wine all on its own, the best winemaking is more of an art. For the 8,000 years or  so that winemaking has been around, humans have become involved in the process. These viticulturists have worked to create the ideal type of grapes for producing the best possible regional varieties of wine.

In searching to grow the perfect grape, the viticulturist has to remember certain indelible facts and choose his or her grapes accordingly. The grower must be aware that each grape requires specific environmental conditions to produce a successful crop for winemaking. The most essential factors are the following:

- Soil Conditions (type, nutrients, acidity, etc.)
- Climate (Temperature, amount of rain, etc.)
- Sunlight (days of sunlight, angle of sunlight, etc.)

The final factor in making wine that does not taste like rot gut is the skill of the vintner. For proper vinification, or the changing of grape juice into wine, the vintner must utilize his or her skills to produce the best wine possible. In the process, the viticulturist must select plants that work into the schedule. Usually, the only grapes selected for wine come from 3rd year vines.

A BRIEF HISTORY OF WINE

Wine has a long and fascinating history that goes back to nearly the dawn of civilization. In fact, the evidence suggests that the production and drinking of wine must go back at least several thousands of years. Early on people discovered the joys of the fermentation process. They learned that grapes could produce an enjoyable nectar that left inhibitions behind and also that by fermenting wine, grape juice could be stored for much longer periods.

The exact date that wine was discovered remains unknown to us. But scholars agree that that by 7,000 BCE cultivated vines were growing in the region of Mount Ararat and in Asia Minor. Civilizations since have continued to develop and refine the process of growing,

[13]

making, and storing wine.

Around 3500 BCE, the Sumerians used irrigation systems to water the vineyards of arid land of Mesopotamia making it able to grow grapes. Since ancient times, winemaking was a well-respected industry. The evidence shows us that the Assyrians, Babylonians and Egyptians all continued the cultivation and production of wine. The trend towards better production methods continued for millennia to follow.

Although the lower classes of the Egyptian people often preferred beer, the high society frequently drank wine. It was considered a sophisticated beverage, one enjoyed by kings. Both the pyramids in the Valley of the Kings and the Valley of the Nobles contain hieroglyphics depicting the growing and the harvesting of grapes. The Egyptians were also the first to label vats of wine and seal them against the negative effects of air. Thus, with Egypt, the preservation of wine began.

The Greeks, in their systematic way, were the first to begin categorizing the different types of grapes. Authors of the time recorded information regarding the techniques and tools used to develop wine. In fact, the Greeks actually invented the pruning knife. They also devised clay wine containers to serve as storage vessels. The Romans took these Greek innovations and techniques further.

More than half a century before Christ turned water into wine the Romans were improving their wine growing techniques and processes. By the time, the Lord arrived there was an obvious difference between good wine and bad. As the Bible reports, hosts often served the best wine first.

We owe much of our knowledge regarding the pruning, fertilization, and reduction of acidity to the Romans. Many of the Roman farmers' practices were recorded by Pliny the Elder. He classified various varieties of grapes and recorded the agricultural terminology for future generations.

Wine can be thought of as one of Rome's lasting gifts to the world for it was the Romans are were first responsible for spreading wine culture throughout Europe and abroad. A number of provinces were known for growing grapes, such as Hispania (Spain), Gaul (France), and Germania (Germany). Interesting enough, these regions still produce quality wines to this day. But the practice wasn't limited to the European mainland. Even England was well documented as a wine producer and consumer. Roman legions stationed there would trade wine for textiles.

Between 500 and 1400 CE, the Christian Church began to cultivate land for their own purposes. They needed sacramental wine to serve Christ's command to remember him as part of the Eucharist. Thus, many monasteries tended to large segments of land devoted primarily to the growing of grapes. At first, monks made basic vintages, but over time, they also began to experiment, improving upon the basic product. The scribes recorded their work for posterity.

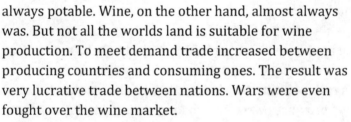

During this period, wine was a common beverage. Water purification methods had not yet been perfected and, therefore, it was not always potable. Wine, on the other hand, almost always was. But not all the worlds land is suitable for wine production. To meet demand trade increased between producing countries and consuming ones. The result was very lucrative trade between nations. Wars were even fought over the wine market.

During the Italian Renaissance wine culture became a culture unto itself. Vineyards flourished. Even as the land developed, the crop expanded. In Elizabethan times, a lord who held rights to the wine trade was almost certainly a very wealthy man. The namesake of a modern sparkling wine, Dom Perignon, was a 17th century Benedictine Monk. He is renowned for truly refining the art of winemaking. He did not discover champagne, but he made it his own.

With the colonization of the New World, settlers brought winemaking with them. Wine is now grown throughout the world. New varieties of grapes emerged as did experimental new flavors. Some met with greater success than others did. Following the period of the Industrial Revolution New World Wines began to make inroads. Wine began to be produced to fulfill demands at all levels of affordability. From there, the need to classify, label, and authenticate wine began to evolve.

Today, top quality wine and cheaper productions both flourish. Each has its own market. Some wines are only crafted for those who truly know the product. Others are created to be enjoyed by all. The current situation embraces wine of all qualities, sweetness levels, and types. There are wines for true connoisseurs as well as the inexpensive box wine that is commonly enjoyed with dinner. The label may bear the name of an ancient and respected vintner. Alternatively, the bottle could be more appealing to the masses, with modern labeling. But, brand isn't everything. We shouldn't judge a wine by its label. Wine may be highly distributed and internationally known, yet still be unpalatable. On the contrary, it can be locally made and quite delectable. In other words, while fancy packaging and a recognizable brand can be an indicator of quality, it isn't always. More than anything else, an enjoyable wine is simply a matter of taste.

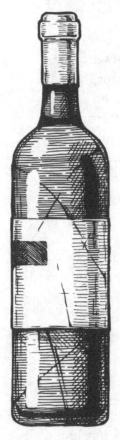

Now that we've given you a short history of wine, we will turn our attention to the core content of this book. Allow this book to serve as your guide to understanding the basic types of wine and common terminology so that you can go from sounding like a beginner to a more refined individual. But it's important to note that this book will not make you an expert and certainly not an oenophile. That is something that requires years of tasting and practice. The appreciation of wine is a life long journey. Yet, even the experts had to start somewhere. Your steps towards wine discovery can be the beginning of a very pleasurable journey. In this book, we will start with the basics, including the answer to that oh so important questions, "how is wine made?"

The short answer is that two things must be present, grapes and fermentation. But we'll look at each of those things further.

Before fermentation even begins, wine must start with good grapes. Essentially, all major grapes come from *Vitis vinifera*. European, Australian, North American, and South American winemakers all use the *Vitis vinifera*, which includes many different varieties of grapes. *Vitis vinifera* can be said to be the original source of most grape varieties. But there are others, such as the American *Vitis labrusa*.

There are more than 8,000 different varieties of grapes. You can make wine from any of them. However, only around 100 grape varieties are commonly enjoyed and discussed by wine lovers.   Among the very basic and popular names of wine you should remember are:

Cabernet Sauvignon
Vitis vinifera. This is arguably the most famous red (black) grape found anywhere in the world. The taste of the grape reflects the character of its locale. It is commonly grown in Bordeaux, Napa Valley, and Chile.

Chardonnay
Vitis vinifera. This is a very adaptable and popular grape. Nevertheless, this green-skinned (white) grape grows in most climates. It has a medium to

high acidity which produces a dry and semi dry white wines. These grapes are grown in Burgundy, Champagne, France, and California.

Chenin blanc
Vitis vinifera. This white grape is also called Pineau de la Loire. It produces white wines. High acidity means that the final product has variable quality. It is grown in the Loire Valley as well as South Africa.

Merlot
Vitis vinifera. Red (black) grapes of this vine produce red wines. Bordeaux reds come from Merlot grapes. It is grown in Bordeaux, Washington State, and Chili.

Muscat
Vitis vinifera. This green (white) grape is also called Muscatel or Muskatel. It is an ancient variety of grape. Muscat grapes can produce frothy and fortified wines. It can be found in Alsace, Piedmont, Greece, Australia, and South Africa. (This family of grapes includes Muscato and Muscat Canelli among others.)

Muscadine
Vitis rotundifolia. A is a grape species native to the southeastern United States. It has been extensively cultivated since the 16th century. The plants are well-adapted to their native warm and humid

climate; they need fewer chilling hours than better known varieties, thriving in summer heat. Both red and white Muscadine wines are medium-bodied with medium to high acidity.

Niagara
Vitis labrusca. This green (white) grape is a north American variety. It is a leading grape in the United States and is found in Canada as well. It's cultivated along the Niagara Peninsula in Ontario and New York.

Pinot Blanc
Vitis vinifera. This white grape is known by another name, Piano. It can be found in Alsace, Luxembourg, and British Columbia.

Pinot Gris
Vitis vinifera. As white grape variety, it produces light, white wines although some can be deeper in color. Usually found in Italy, France, and Australia.

Pinot Noir
Vitis vinifera. A red (black) grape, that is difficult to cultivate. But it thrives in Burgundy, Sonoma, Oregon, and New Zealand.

Riesling

Vitis vinifera. A white grape that produces both sweet and dry wines. Grown primarily in Germany and France.

Sangiovese

Vitis vinifera. A red Italian grape that can produce full-bodied wines. Most commonly grown in Tuscany.

Sauvignon Blanc

Vitis vinifera. This green-skinned (white) grape is highly acidic. Produces a wine with zing. Grown in a variety of regions.

Sémillon

Vitis vinifera. A golden-skinned (white) grape, not always used alone. It is often combined with Sauvignon to produce dry wines. Usually grown in California and Washington.

Syrah

Vitis vinifera. A dark-skinned grape from Rhône. Syrah is high in both tannins and acidity and used in varietal and blending. It is also high in popularity.

Tempranillo
Vitis vinifera. The noble grape of Spain. It is a red (black) grape, that produces a full bodied red wine. The popular regions for growing it are located in Spain, South America, and the United States.

Zinfandel
Vitis vinifera. With its origins in Croatia, this grape is high in sugar content, and is often used to create sweet blush wines.

These varieties of grapes are the some of the most common varieties of wine grapes. You should know their names and the type of wine they produce. You should also be able to differentiate the white grapes from the black grapes even though the color of the grapes is neither white nor black. As we discuss later, wine, despite the grapes color, is classified as white, red or rosé. But first, we will discuss how we get from grape to bottle.

FERMINTATION

Fermentation is the process by which the grape juice turns into wine. There is a simple formulation for fermentation. It is:

Sugar + Yeast = Alcohol + Carbon Dioxide

The fermentation process begins when the grapes are

crushed and ends when all of the sugar has been converted or the alcohol levels reach about 15%. At this point, the alcohol will kill off the yeast.

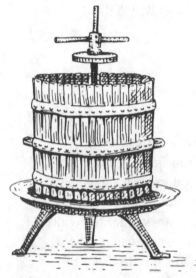

Sugar is naturally present in the ripe grape because of a process known as photosynthesis. Sugar is what gives ordinary grapes their sweetness. Yeast also exists naturally and can be seen as the white bloom on the grape skin. Although the fermentation process will naturally occur because of the existing presence of yeast and sugar in crushed grapes, the natural yeast is not always used to begin the fermentation process.

Today there are many isolated strains of pure yeast that can contribute something unique to the style of wine. During production the carbon dioxide dissipates into the air, except when making Champagne or another sparkling wine. In this case the gas will be retained through a process that we will discuss later.

CHAPTER 2: MAKING WINE

"Beer is made by men, wine by God."

— Martin Luther

We've already discussed how there are essentially two things necessary to create any wine: grapes and fermentation. We also discussed how, over the ages, people have refined and improved the winemaking process. Here, we'll explain how wine is made today as that insight will help you to further appreciate the finished product.

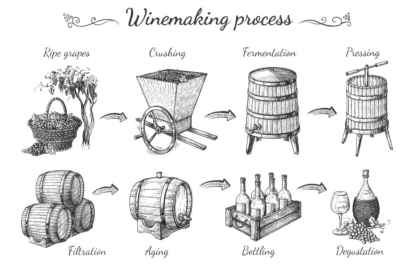

Winemaking process

Ripe grapes · Crushing · Fermentation · Pressing
Filtration · Aging · Bottling · Degustation

THE RIGHT GRAPES; THE RIGHT AREA

If one were to delve into winemaking, the first thing he
would consider is what grapes are right for the area. Like
any other agricultural products, grapes require specific
growing conditions. Just as you wouldn't grow pineapples
in Minnesota, you wouldn't try to grow grapes in
Antarctica. There are specific limitations on the area
where grapes can be grown and the variety of grapes that
can be grown there.

Some of these limitations, as we touched on previously,
include the length of the growing season, the amount of
sunlight the area receives, the angle of the sun, the regions
average temperature, and the amount of rainfall. The most
important concern is the soil. Adequate drainage is
definitely a prerequisite. Each variety is unique, so these
factors play a role in whether or not the grapes ripen
properly. They need a proper sugar/acid balance to
produce a quality wine. The little differences separate the
average wine for the spectacular.

It's well known that certain grape varieties produce better
wines when planted in particular locations. In most cases,
red grapes need longer growing seasons than white
grapes. Accordingly, they are usually planted in warmer
locations, such as Spain, Portugal, and Napa Valley. In
colder regions, such as Germany, you'll find that most
vineyards contain white grapes.

[26]

THE PROPER TIME TO HARVEST

It matters when the grapes are picked. They are harvested when they reach the proper sugar to acid ratio. Exactly what this ratio is depends on the site of wine that the vintner wants to produce. If you pick the grapes too soon, the grape will be tart and acidic. Later, they will be sweeter. Each month of sun gives more sugar to the grape thanks to photosynthesis. In wine making terms, the brix rises with each month. Brix is the winemaker's measure of sugar in the grapes.

Weather, too, has an effect on the harvest. An early frost may reduce yields. Rain just before harvest will swell the grapes with water, diluting the juice making thin wines.

PROTECTING AGAINST ADVERSE WEATHER

The vintner must protect his crop from conditions that can be problematic to the grape quality. When adverse weather affects the yield a number of counter measures may be used. Some are used while the grape is still on the vine, but for others it's part of the winemaking process.

Problem	Resulting Problem	Possible Solutions
Not Enough Sun	Underripe Grapes; Vegetal Character; High Acidity	Adding sugar to the must
Too Much Sun	Overripe Grapes; Prune Character	Addition of water to the must
Too Much Rain	Watery Wines	Relocation of vineyard
Not Enough Rain	Scorched Grapes	Irrigation
Frost	Reduced Yield	Protect from frost with wind machines, sprinklers, or heaters

OTHER CONSIDERATIONS

Other factors play a role in the development of a fine wine. Things such as the amount of tannins, the acidity of the soil and grapes, as well as the age and vintage of the wine are all important factors in determining the quality of the finished wine.

THE GRAPES' COLORS

The color of wine comes entirely from the grape skins. When the skins are removed immediately after picking, the wine has no resulting color and will therefore be a white wine. Many grapes red grapes are used to produce white wine. And likewise, some white wines, such as White Zinfandel, are produced with red grapes. So, the color of the grapes is not as important as other factors. Tannins

Tannin is a natural preservative and is present in the skins, pits, and stems of the grapes. Another source of tannin is the barrels in which some wines are aged or fermented. Generally speaking, red wines have a higher level of tannic flavor than whites because the grapes used in making red wine are usually left to ferment with their skins. Wines with high levels of tannins can be described as astringent, and can taste bitter.

ACIDITY

All wine has some level of acidity. White wines often have more perceivable acidity than reds. That is why winemakers often try to balance it with fruit flavors. An acidic wine can taste sour.

AGE AND VINTAGE

The vintage is the year in which the grapes were harvested. The quality of a particular vintage is dependent upon the weather conditions of the year. This is different from the age of the wine.

The age of the wine is just like yours, it increases every year. But it's worth noting that it's a common misconception that all wines improve with age. That's simply untrue. Most wines should be consumed within a year of bottling. Some do get better, but that is the exception rather than the rule.

So what makes a wine worth aging? Well, the color and the grape matter. Red wines generally age longer than whites. This is due to their tannin content which acts as a preservative. The vintage and region of production also play a factor as does the method by which the wine was made. The longer the wine remains in contact with the skin or is aged in oak, the more tannin it will contain.

HARVESTING THE GRAPES

Growing grapes is the just first step of the winemaking process. Once the grapes are ready, they have to be picked. Most vineyards start by collecting the white grapes first and then move to red varietals. The grapes will be collected in bins or lugs before being transported to the crushing pad. This is where the process of turning grapes into juice and subsequently into wine begins.

The method of collecting the grapes depends upon the vineyards preferences. The grapes are either cut from the vine by human hands with shears or they could be removed from the vine by a machine. Some vineyards elect to pick the grapes during the day, while others will collect them at night to maximize efficiency, beat the heat, and collect grapes at stable sugar levels.

At this point in the process, the grapes are still attached to their stems. Some leaves and sticks will also remain attached. But these will all be removed in the next step of the wine making process.

CRUSHING THE GRAPES

No matter how or when the grapes were picked, they all get crushed in some fashion, but first they will be sent to the destemmer. The destemmer is a machine that does exactly what it sounds like; it removes the stems from the clusters and lightly crushes the grapes. From here, what happens next depends on what kind of wine is being produced.

When making white wine, after the grapes are crushed, the white grapes will be transferred to the press. The press is another piece of winemaking equipment that does exactly what it sounds like. All of the grapes are pressed to extract the juice and leave behind the grape skins. The juice will be moved to the tanks so that the sediment can settle. After settling, the juice is then "racked", which means it is filtered before being pumped into another tank to insure that no sediment remains. When the fermentation starts, we want to be working with pure juice.

The process for red wine is similar. Red wine grapes (sometimes called "black" grapes) are commonly destemmed and lightly crushed. The difference is that when making red wine, the grape skins stay with the juice and they'll skip the settlement tank. Instead they'll both the juice and stems will end up in a vat to begin the fermentation process. The skins, give the wine its color.

As discussed in the first chapter, fermentation is the process by which sugar converts into alcohol. There are a lot of techniques and technologies used depending on the type of grapes being used. But to keep this simple, we will just discuss the most common methods.

For all three types of wine, yeast is added to the vats to speed up the fermentation process. With red wines, the carbon dioxide that is released during fermentation causes the grape skins to rise to the surface. The wine producer must push the "cap" back down several times a day to keep the skins in contact with the juice. Alternatively, they can pump the juice over the cap to keep the skins in contact with the juice. Either way, it works to promote fermentation of the juice with saturated grape skins. Some winemakers will use yeast nutrients to speed and strengthen the fermentation process. After fermentation the grapes of the red wines will finally be pressed.

Most wines are aged to some degree. After racking to clarify the wine, the reds will be aged for several months in barrels. The barrel choice depends on the wine, but both French oak and American oak are common choices for red wines. For some wines, steel, used, or charred barrels are used, instead of new wood barrels. Aging helps the wine flavors become more intense.

[33]

The aging process can last several months to several years. It all depends on the type of wine that the winemaker wants to develop. Once he feels that the wine has reached its full expression, it will be bottled. Some whites are ready to be bottled within a few months, while most dry red wines need a year and a half to two years. As some wineries, the bottling is done by hand. At others, the bottling process is completely automated.

CHAPTER 3: THE TYPES OF WINE

"Men are like wine-some turn to vinegar, but the best improve with age."

--Pope John XXIII

There are a number of ways to classify and group wines. They can broadly be classified by color, by sweetness, or by type. We'll describe each of the methods of classifying wine below. Knowing how to describe wine can help you identify and select one that fits your unique tastes.

COLOR CLASSIFICATIONS

As mentioned before, grapes are essentially divided into one of two basic types: white and black. This does not indicate either the actual color of the grapes or the wine produced by the grapes. It is simply a method to classify the grapes. Wine, in turn, is divided into various styles. These are white, red, and rosé.

White wine is not actually white. When you are looking at a white wine, you will find that it is a golden yellow or even pale in color. White wine is simply describes wine that is lacking red or pink pigment. In other words, white wine is wine that is not red, or rosé.

White wine can be made from "white" grapes. But white grapes are not actually white. They are green, yellow, or sometimes a pinkish-yellow. Like the white wine they produce, a white grape is a grape that is not something else. A white grape is one that is not dark red, bluish, or black.

But a white wine need not come from white grapes. A vintner can also make white wine from the juice of red (black) grapes. As mentioned in the last chapter, the juice of the red or black grapes does not contain pigmentation. White wines are frequently served before dinner. They may replace a cocktail. White wine is also commonly served at parties and in bars. They are often enjoyed on hot days. They should be served chilled, but not cold.

White wines worthy of note are Chardonnay, Pinot Blanc, Riesling, and Sauvignon Blanc.

RED WINE

Obviously, red wine is red in color, just as its name implies. The source of the color is the red or bluish grapes from which it is made. The grapes are sometimes called "black." All red wines come from black grapes.

In terms of taste, red wines tend to be more complex than whites and offer a greater variety. Red wines may be full, medium, or light bodied. They are not usually served as a self-standing drink, but are often paired with meals. Unlike white wines, reds are usually served near room temperature.

Red wines worthy of mention include Cabernet, Merlot, and Pinot Noir.

ROSÉ WINE

Like Red Wines, Rosé Wines are made with black grapes. They are sometimes called blush wines, but are not to be confused with red wines. Blush wines are comparable to white wines. They often have a sweet taste. Rosés are fine to drink alone or with meals, which in some ways make it the all-purpose wine, but they do need to be chilled before drinking.

Examples worth trying include Pink Merlot and White Zinfandel.

DRY, SEMI-SWEET OR SWEET

There are other ways to view or classify wine. One of the most useful ways is to categorize the wine by style or

Wine Sweetness Chart

Reds

Dry
— sangiovese
— tempranillo
— cabernet sauvignon
— pinot noir
— syrah

Medium
— merlot
— malbec
— garnacha
— zinfandel

Sweet
— lambrusco dolce
— port

Whites

muscadet — Dry
sauvignon blanc —
pinot gris —
chardonnay —
chenin blanc —
viognier — Medium
torrontes —
gewurztraminer —
riesling —
moscato — Sweet
ice wine —

flavor of wine. Wine style encompasses the level of sweetness. Varying acidity levels of the grapes results in different textures. Wine is, in these terms, can be described as dry, semi-sweet or sweet.

DRY WINE

Dry, in wine terminology, is the opposite of sweet. So Dry Wines are wines, which are not sweet. In these wines, the sugars have been fully fermented. The acidity is more noticeable. There are levels of dryness indicated by the sugar levels of wine. The lowest levels represent the driest wines, the highest levels the sweetest.

The pH level of wine is another major factor in determining how dry a wine may be. A pH level of between 2.8 to 3.3 would indicate a dry wine. But even the complete fermentation of grapes does not reduce the sugar content to zero. This is because when the alcohol level reaches a certain point, it will kill the yeast leaving some sugar intact.

The wines with the lowest sugars include most Chardonnays and Cabernet Sauvignon wines. Other dry wines include many white German dry wines such as Pinot Gris and Riesling. All red wines are considered dry.

SEMI-SWEET WINE

There are not wines that are completely dry. They are sometimes called off-dry. We refer to those wines as Semi-sweet wines. Semi-sweet Wines fall between the categories of dry and sweet. White wines fall can fall into this semi-sweet category, or they may be sweet or semi-sweet. Blush wines are a perfect example of semi-sweet wines. The German Spätlese is a perfect example of a semi-sweet wine.

SWEET WINE

Sweet Wines are those with the highest sugar levels. They are unmistakably sweet and more akin to juice. The process to create sweet wine can follow several methods. White grapes are allowed to become very ripe and sugar is often added.

Grapes are dried in a specific method using boxes or mats. Sometimes, the vintner even permits the grapes to freeze on the vine.

Sweet and semi-sweet wines can also be created in other ways. Sweet wines also include dessert wines, ice wines, and port wines. Like the other classifications, there are multiple variations on sweet wine. But the important part to remember is that sugar level and acidity each contribute to the depth of the sweetness. A high sugar level can be balanced by a higher level of acidity. Common sweet wines include Moscato, White Zinfandel, and Riesling.

TABLE, SPARKLING, FORTIFIED, OR DESSERT

There is another way to classify wine—by type. Under this system, wines can be grouped into the following categories: Table Wine, Sparkling Wine, Dessert Wine and Fortified Wine. This describes a way of looking at wine. It is based on the alcoholic content of the finished wine. Table wine contains 8-15% alcohol. Table wine is also called still wine. This is the type of wine that people most often drink. Table wines are typically dry or semi-sweet in style. Table wines come in all colors: Red, White or even Rosé.

Sparkling wine contains 8 to 12% alcohol. What makes it different from table wine is the presence of carbon dioxide. Carbon dioxide is a natural byproduct of fermentation.   In the production of sparkling wines, the gas is retained. As a result, the wine is bubbles. The most well-known sparkling wine is Champagne.

Fortified wine has higher alcohol content, from 17 to 22%. This wine is created by adding additional alcohol before or after fermentation. Port and Sherry are both fortified wines.

Dessert wines are super sweet. They contain around 14% alcohol and are almost always the product of light-skinned grapes. Freezing the grape on the vine is common practice. Canada's ice wines are one example of dessert wines.

CONCLUSION

Before becoming an expert on wine and winemaking, you really need to start with a very basic comprehension of the subject. By now, you should be able to name some of the most common grapes and types of wine as well as the characteristics of each. From these basics, your knowledge can grow. But as you'll see, the debate over wine is one that seems to always be in vogue.

CHAPTER 4: NEW WORLD OR OLD WORLD

"Accept what life offers you and try to drink from every cup. All wines should be tasted; some should only be sipped, but with others, drink the whole bottle."

— Paulo Coelho, Brida

TRADITIONAL DIFFERENCES

For centuries one debate has continued. Where does the best wine come from? Wine connoisseurs disagree on what country produces the best wine. The growth of the wine industry in the New World has only intensified this debate. So, which wine is better – Old World or New World? Well, the answer is that it depends.

Depends on what? It depends on a whole variety of factors. It depends upon whether you like the technological or traditional approach to winemaking. It depends on upon whether you prefer fruity flavors over earthy wines. Which is better depends entirely upon your personal taste and perception.

Actually, as the market for wine becomes global and opportunities for the exchange of knowledge advance, the division between Old World and New World wines is no longer easily defined. The New and Old Worlds have fewer differences than they have in years past. Viticulture technology and an increasingly connected world have reduced the degree of difference between Old and New Worlds.

OLD WORLD WINE

We use the term Old World Wines to describe the wines produced by the traditional winemaking countries of Europe. France, Italy, and Spain continue to dominate in the area of wine production. I'd also include wines from Greece, Germany, Portugal, and Austria in my listing of Old World wines. There is an aura of mystery surrounding the production of European wines.

France and Italy are both known for their romantic lands and for many people wine is where the romance starts. There is the ancient heritage of the Greek and Roman techniques that exist in Europe. In many cases, centuries of knowledge and even the vineyards themselves are passed down through families. European winemakers can often point to their ancestors as the source of their knowledge; much like the secret family recipe is shared here. Their family methods transition from one generation to the next.

Tradition is one aspect of the Old World production methods. Established traditions are rarely broken and the processes of making and aging wine conform to certain expectations. In these ways, Old World winemaking has remained virtually unchanged over the centuries. Established traditions combine with laws governing certain aspects of wine production e.g. combination of grape varieties, to create a consistency. Old World wines stay true to classic winemaking. Wine drinkers around the world can name the most famous wine regions: Burgundy, Piedmont, Mosel-Saar, Champaign, and La Rioja. These regions consistently produce incredible vintages.

Yet, despite consistently good production, there remains

variety. The French call this Terroir. Terroir explains the impact that soil, light, slope, altitude, and climate have on the grape harvest. These differences account for the subtle differences of the wine and its dry nature.

For wine snobs, Old World wines have appeal. With a rich history spanning thousands of years into the past, the Old World must certainly create fine wine. At least that's what they believe. The reliance on culture and family names contribute to the appeal. For many, a wine bearing an Old World name must certainly be good. But is that

[45]

always the case?

NEW WORLD WINE

New World Wines are the fresh contenders. We use this phrase to describe wine that is produced anywhere but Europe. We include the ostentatious labels from the United States, the creative combinations from Chili, and bold flavors of Australia. Winemakers in the New World have a different approach to winemaking.

The most significant mark of distinction with New World wines is the reliance on technology. The New World, after all, has few standing traditions to hold on to. Many have less than a hundred years of winemaking history and have no heritage to uphold. So the word that defines New World winemaking is innovation.

Technology, science, and innovation are the cornerstones of New World wines. California vintners make use of technology and experiment with hybrid grapes. Canada is the premier place for new categories, like ice wines. The New World is driven not, by tradition, but by a determination to make something new. Discovery is the defining trait of New World wines. This holds true for products and technological innovation.

With fewer regulations, New World wines often

experiment with blends of different varietals. Even Old World grapes produce unique flavors in New World soils. Vineries in the Eastern United States are using Native American varieties such as *Vitis labrusca* and *Vitis rotundifolia*. In Missouri, Chardonnay becomes Chardonel. The South produces Muscadine wine. In Australia, Syrah grapes are now Shiraz grapes. They produce an excellent table wine. Australia also makes a very popular Yellow Tail wine. It is popular worldwide. New Zealand is gaining marks for its Sauvignon Blanc.

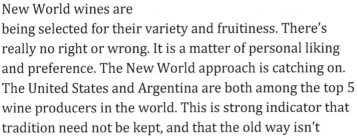

Many may still choose Old World wines for their more subtle flavor and reserved style, but New World wines are being selected for their variety and fruitiness. There's really no right or wrong. It is a matter of personal liking and preference. The New World approach is catching on. The United States and Argentina are both among the top 5 wine producers in the world. This is strong indicator that tradition need not be kept, and that the old way isn't necessarily the best.

DIFFERENT REGIONS; DIFFERENT TASTES

The world is full of incredible places. But few are more beautiful than wine country, wherever you are. These regions produce so many different types of wines. And they are all available for you to taste.

Wine culture has often been filled with local, national, and continental snobbery. But the likes of others don't have to define you. The only way to know what you truly prefer is to explore wines from around the world.   Both the New and Old Worlds have something to offer. Below you'll discover a few of the world's finest wine producing regions.

> **Argentina:** Here the region of production is Mendoza where both white and red wines are grown. There are excellent examples of Malbec wines, a French variety from Bordeaux.

> **Australia:** This country produces more white wine than red. Try the Shiraz. This is a region that was once looked down on, but is now producing quality vintages.

> **Austria:** White wines also dominate here. The countries four wine producing regions put out a

good variety of wines. Maybe try a Grüner Veltliner, which is comparable to Sauvignon Blanc.

Canada: Canada is a new producer of wines, best known for its Ice Wines.

Chile: Mainly fine white wines. If you want something special, find a Carménère.

France: France is home to many incredible wine regions. They include Alsace, Loire Valley, Bordeaux Burgundy, and Champagne.

Germany: Known for incredible whites. The Riesling grape is the grape to try. Another famous wine from Germany is Liebfraumilch, a medium-dry white wine.

Italy: Native grape varieties produce red and white wines. There are at least 20 wine producing regions, such as Piedmont, Veneto, and Tuscany. The wine to try is Chianti.

New Zealand: Produces both red and white wines. You've probably heard of Marlborough. Others include Martinborough and Hawke's Bay. You'll probably want to try a Sauvignon Blanc.

Portugal: Creates port wines and medium Rosés. If you want to dry something different, look for the Vinho Verde, a white table wine.

South Africa: Primarily produces white wines. Known for the Chenin Blanc.

Spain: Red wine territory. The one to try is Rioja.

United States: Wines are both red and white. A unique grape found there is called the Norton.

CONCLUSION

Some choose the old classics of Europe; others find their favorites among the new classics. The great debate surrounding where the best wines are made continues. While the Old World relies on culture and tradition, the New World utilizes technology and experimentation.

The basis of a good wine remains good grapes. The nature of the environment and the ability of the vintner continue to define the wine. But the decision as to who makes the best wine remains with the individual. More important than the opinion of any critic is your own personal preference.

CHAPTER 5: ATTENDING A WINE TASTING

"One not only drinks the wine, one smells it, observes it, tastes it, sips it and--one talks about it."

- King Edward VII

DISCOVERING THE RIGHT WINE

Any true wine lover has only one way to enhance his understanding of wine. By trying as many wines as possible. Reading only covers the academic side of wine, but tasting is more enjoyable. A bit of each is necessary to truly embrace the wine culture.

 If you want to embrace the philosophy, of learning by tasting, then you'll need to get out there and taste the available wines. Depending upon your financial situation, location, and willingness to explore, this could either be an easy task or a difficult one.

There are a number of ways that you can approach the subject. But in any case, the tasting can be broken down into five simple steps: Evaluate the Color, Swirl, Smell, Taste, and Savor.

But before you can do that, you'll want to find a place to indulge. Beyond, trying what your favorite restaurants have available, there are a number of other options. The first step is to find out where tasting events take place. Common hosts of wine tastings include:

Local Wineries. A great way to get started is by tasting any locally produced wines. Getting acquainted with wines produced in your region may be a less daunting task than taking on a whole world worth of wine right up front. Most wineries are happy to pour a flight of their selections. And you might want to ask if they will be hosting a wine and dine event with their wine maker. Many do and it's a great way to learn more about the winemaking process and find out more about different wines. They may also teach you to pair particular wines with certain foods.

Wine Courses. Many community colleges offer continuing education courses in wine. Not only is this a great way to make friends with other people who are interested in the wine culture, but it's a great starting point for diving deeper into what makes a quality wine. Vineries often offer similar courses; you'll just have to ask. These types of courses, whether offered through a college or a winery, may involve more than just wine tasting. Some provide a solid foundation in the science of viticulture and the economics of the wine industry.

Wine Sellers. You're local wine dealers may have special events where they show off their distributor's products. This is an excellent way to try a particular wine before you decide to spend your money on it.   Many high end liquor stores offer wine tastings on regular basis.

Visit a Wine Region. Most American's life within a day's drive of one of our wine producing regions. By making a day trip out of it, you can visit several different wineries at once. Many wineries offer tours of their grounds. Depending on the time of year that you go, this is a great way to see wine making first hand.

Online Wine Education. If you can't attend a tasting in person, you can always host one at home. And there are plenty of online courses to point you in the right direction. Both free and paid courses are available. A listing of them can be found in a later chapter.

Before you attend a tasting, you should be aware of the

type of tasting. There are two common types of tastings, vertical and horizontal, as well as introductory flights. Vertical refers to a tasting in which all the wines presented are different vintages of the same wine. Horizontal tastings involve trying a single vintage from several different wineries. Introductory tastings, which are more common, select a variety of wines from the sweet to dry. This type of tasting may be the most useful in helping you determine your wine preferences.

All three types of tastings will help you understand wines. And all of them may be conducted blind. A blind tasting means that the labels on the bottles will be concealed in some way. I've also seen restaurants present the wines to their servers this way to educate them on the available  selections. This prevents any potential bias or preconception from influencing the perception of the presented wines.

Another interesting type of tasting I've seen is one where an inexpensive wine was blindly tested against a more expensive one of the same type. In many cases the sample group selected the less expensive wine as the better one. This goes to show you that personal preference and not

[54]

the price tag is the most important factor.

Whatever type of wine tasting you decide to attend, be sure that you understand some basic wine tasting skills and etiquette.

HOW TO TASTE WINE

We told you that the steps for tasting wine can be broken down into five simple steps: evaluate the color, swirl the wine, smell it, taste it, and then savor it. But what do we mean by that?

COLOR

To evaluate the color of the wine, you'll want to observe the color in a well light area and you may want to old the glass in front of a white background. A napkin or white tablecloth would do the trick.

The color can tell may tell you a lot about the wines age. A younger white while may have a pale yellow or even green color while an older one may be gold or even brown. When it comes to reds, younger wines tend to have a purple or ruby color, but trend towards brick red and then brown as they age. As white wine ages it gains color. Reds, on the other hand, lose color with age.

Age isn't the only factor. There are a few reasons why a white wine may have more color. Different varieties give off different colors. Or, aging in wood can affect the color.

SWIRL

Before we even smell the wine, we swirl it in the glass. But, why? It allows oxygen to get into the wine and releases esters, ethers, aldehydes, and other aromatics to combine with the oxygen to release more of the wine's bouquet. A wines bouquet is the overall smell of the wine. Put another way, the act of swirling the wine aerates it and releases more aroma.

When you first begin, you might want to place your hand over the glass when you swirl it so that when you go to smell the wine you'll experience a stronger bouquet.

SMELL

This is arguably the most important part of wine tasting. After all, the average human has around 5,000 taste buds but there are more than 10,000 different smells in the world. Furthermore, people can perceive just five tastes, but they can identify more than two thousand different scents. You should definitely take a moment to take in the different aromas and see what you can identify.

The following chart shows some of the classic ways of describing individual grape varieties. See if your personal experience with each wine is detects the same aromatic notes.

Wine	Aroma / Notes
Chardonnay	Buttery; Crisp Apple
Riesling	Green Apple
Sauvignon Blanc	Grapefruit
Rhône	Black Pepper
Zinfandel	Blackberry
Cabernet Sauvignon	Chocolate
Pinot Noir	Cherry

Not only can your sense of smell help you to identify the wine and notice some of its subtleties, but it can also help you recognize some of the common defects of wine. It's a simple fact that wine can go bad in time or that there are occasional problems with corks.

The chart below lists some of the common negative smells

that can be detected in bad wine and the causes.

Negative Scent	Cause
Sherry	Oxidation*
Sulfur	Excessive sulfur dioxide**
Vinegar	Too much acetic acid
Wet, Moldy Smell	Defective cork

*Real Sherry is intentionally made with controlled oxidation.
**All wines contain some sulfur dioxide as a byproduct of fermentation.

TASTE

For many people tasting wine means to just take a sip and swallow. But that doesn't begin to create the experience that wine should bring. Your mouth is full of taste buds that are ready to perceive the flavor. One who truly appreciates the vine will take a moment to allow the flavor to flow across their taste buds.

By keeping the wine in your mouth for a few seconds before swallowing, the wine warms up, sending the bouquet up through the nasal passage to the olfactory bulb. Scientists say that up to 90 percent of what we experience as taste actually comes through smell.

When we taste something, we can only perceive five tastes through our taste buds, the rest comes from the rich aroma of wine. The flavors that our tongue can detect are sweet, sour, bitter, salty, and savory. Any bitterness in wine is usually created by a high alcohol and tannin content. Sweetness occurs when residual sugars remain after fermentation. Occasionally you may even taste hints of an included sour fruit. Each wine is unique.

What we perceive as taste isn't limited to what we can perceive with our taste buds or nose. We also detect a number of sensations that contribute to our overall perspective of the wine. We detect acidity at the sides of the tongue, the cheek area, and the back of the throat. We experience sensations of tannin in the middle of the tongue. You may notice this with wines aged in would, just as you do with many teas.

Even after we swallow, we experience an aftertaste. The overall taste and balance of the wine remains for a moment. All of these things contribute to the experience and it's why we encourage you to savor the wine.

Take a moment to think about what you just experienced and enjoy the impressions the wine brings. This is what we mean by savoring the wine.

You may even want to ask yourself a few questions about the flavor. Here's a few examples of things to think about to absorb the moment.

- Would you describe the wine as light, medium, or full bodied? (Did you pick up on any other flavors?)
- What was the strongest part of the wine? (Was it the sugar, the acidity, the tannins, or fruit flavors?)
- Did the wine seem well balanced? (Was the bouquet pleasurable?)
- What foods would you pair with the wine? (What occasions?)
- Did it invoke any memories? (Or remind you of anything else?)

These are the kinds of questions that will help you discover your preferences and refine your taste. This experience is the one that matters. More than your knowledge about the wine, what is important is whether or not you enjoyed a particular wine.

It could be compared to browsing an art gallery. Your first impression is a good indicator of whether or not you like something. Once a particular piece catches your eyes, you want to know more. What feelings does it invoke? What inspired the work? Who was the craftsman that put it together? Is there a story behind the painting? It's very much the same way with wine.

PROPER ETIQUETTE

Wine isn't just a beverage, it's a culture. Before you sign up for a tasting, you should recall that there is a certain type of etiquette is expected. Like any social gathering, the exact protocol may vary some based on the atmosphere.

This may vary according to the protocol and/or atmosphere of the tasting. Generally speaking though, there are two universal rules.

1. You shouldn't smoke or wear any scent. Perfumes and cigarettes distract from the natural bouquets of the wine. As we discussed, taking in the aroma of the wine is an important part of the overall experience.

2. You shouldn't volunteer your opinion on the wine before everyone has had a chance to try it. Each person should have the opportunity to experience the wine selection for him or herself.

[61]

Aside from those essential rules, basic common courtesy is expected. I usually refrain from talking too technically in the tasting room because it can seem like I am showing off. And I'm not there to show my knowledge, but to learn something and maybe discover something new. Be sociable and likable. No one likes a snob.

I often get asked about other protocols in the tasting rooms. Like should you tip? Well that depends. Some wineries don't accept them. "It's a tasting room, not a bar." I've heard them say. But other times compensating a good host seems like the appropriate thing to do. My advice is to pay attention to what others do and do what they do.

Another age old question, is should you spit or swallow? Older advice advises you to spit your wine out so as not to ruin your palate before your next pour. But there's really no hard or fast rule. So I say go ahead and swallow. It's not all about learning and it's ok to drink at little and have some fun. I mean what's the point of wine if you can't enjoy it? Plus, spitting a good wine back into a glass always seemed like a waste to me.

Wine tasting should be fun. It may seem serious, but the whole idea was developed to be an enjoyable learning experience. It's a chance to rub elbows with people from all walks of life. I've been to vineyards that are quite formal and others that cater to hippies. Whatever the atmosphere, it's supposed to be an enjoyable experience. And, attending tastings is a great way to measure how much you've learned. And, sometimes, how much more there is to discover. For me, at least, I find human history in every glass.

Types of Wine Glasses

Red Wine   White Wine   Champagne   Brandy

Dry white   Sweet white   Rich white   Sparkling wine

Rose   Light red   Medium red   Bold red   Dessert

Wine Styles

CHAPTER 6: ONLINE WINE EDUCATION

"A person with increasing knowledge and sensory education may derive infinite enjoyment from wine."

-Earnest Hemingway

If you want to take your knowledge one step further, online wine courses are a great way to do that. Sure, they are no substitute for real life tasting, but they can teach you a variety of subjects regarding the growing, cultivation, production, and appreciation of wine. So here, I've chosen to highlight some of the better programs.

SHORT COURSES

Even short courses can be beneficial to you when it comes to learning about wine. Sometimes, they give you a broad overview on a specific topic, such as different wines, the wine making process, or the wine regions. If you want to explore wine beyond this book, a short course is a good place to start. Sometimes, these courses are set up much like a tasting would be. In those cases, you'll want to purchase the wines from the course and follow along at home.

WINE FOLLY'S WINE STYLES TASTING COURSE

This is a hands-on tasting course, designed by Madeline Puckette, will give you an overview of wine while training your palate. This is the online equivalent of a wine tasting. The course offers a selection of curated regional wines, tasting tips, and a guided video experience.

It can help you become more confident in discussing wine and avoid feeling lost when looking at a wine list. Plus, it's a good way to begin expanding your palate.

Link: https://shop.winefolly.com/pages/online-wine-course

Course Level: Beginner

Course Length: 2+ Hours of video.

Cost: $19 USD

WSET LEVEL 2 CERTIFICATE COURSE

This is a five week long certification course from the Napa Valley Wine Academy that results in earning a WSET Level 2 Certificate. WSET is the Wine & Sprit Education Trust. The course includes a six bottle (187ml bottles) wine tasting kit designed to accompany the course. The wines in the kit were carefully selected by Master of Wine Peter Marks and the head of Napa Valley Wine Academy, Catherine Bugue.

You'll use this kit to actively taste the examples along with your instructor during the two live wine tasting webinars that are included with the online course. This course provides a great opportunity to calibrate your palate. You'll have to successfully complete an online exam to earn your certification. One examination credit is included with the course.

Link:

https://napavalleywineacademy.com/product/wset-level-2-5-week-online-course/

Course Level: Beginner

Course Length: 6 hours of Video, Two Live Webinars, plus sample exams.

Cost: $599 USD

CERTIFIED SPECIALIST OF WINE COURSE

This is a nine week course from the San Francisco Wine School lead by Master Sommelier David Glancy. It covers wine tasting, terminology, composition, chemistry, and common flaws. It goes over reading labels, relevant laws, and the different wine regions. If you want to learn about the different regional wines, this is the course to take. There are seven modules that focus on different wine making regions.

You'll have to buy your own wines to follow along, but this course is taught as a live webinar series, which means that there is peer interaction that goes beyond just watching videos. This course is designed to prepare you for the proctored CSW exam. A CSW is a Certified Specialist of Wine as recognized by the Society of Wine Educators. It comes with a certificate and pin. This is an industry recognized certification and is great for resumes.

Link:
https://sanfranciscowineschool.com/products/certified-specialist-of-wine-online

Course Level: Intermediate

Course Length: 9 Weeks

Cost: 1095 USD

WINE SCHOLAR GUILD COURSES

Other courses worth looking at are the Wine Scholar Guild courses. The also require passing a certification exam, but are perfect for students who wish to specialize in the wine of a specific country. These are advanced programs that provide in-depth information on the wines of France, Italy, or Spain. After successful completion of the program, you will be able to call yourself a French Wine Scholar, an Italian Wine Scholar, or a Spanish Wine Scholar.

You'll be encouraged to buy wines from a recommended list and work through modules featuring a study manual, quizzes, digital study materials, and an exam. When you pass the program, you'll be presented with a certificate and pin.

Link:
https://www.winescholarguild.org/programs/wine-scholar-programs.html

Course Level: Advanced

Course Length: 15 Week Instructor-led format, 12 Online Study Modules, 8 Live Webinars

Cost: $790

THE UNIVERSITY OF ADELAIDE'S WORLD OF WINE

This course will teach you the principles and practices of growing grapes and making wine. It's perfect for both wine novices and seasoned oenophiles. By the time you are through, you'll be able to confidently describe wine appearance, aroma, flavor and taste.

If you want to learn about the attributes that make wine so enjoyable, this course has you covered. You see how decisions in the vineyard and winery both contribute to the final product. This course goes over vineyard management practices and various winemaking techniques. Best part? This course is free. But if you want a verified certificate, it'll cost $199.

Link:
https://www.edx.org/course/world-of-wine-from-grape-to-glass

Course Level: Beginner

Course Length: 6 Weeks, Self-Paced Video

Cost: Free or $199 USD for a verified course certificate

LONG COURSES

If wine is your calling, you may want to look into more formalized education. As indicated by the previous listing, colleges are beginning to jump on the winemaking bandwagon. If it is your passion, even online, you can receive a world-class university level education in wine making.

UC DAVIS - WINE MAKING CERTIFICATE PROGRAM

If you want to take your knowledge to the next level, college courses are available. UC Davis offers an internationally acclaimed Winemaking Certificate Program, which will enable you to pursue your passion for winemaking. The course is designed for those in the commercial winemaking. The goal of the program is to provide a scientific and technical frame work for wine production, with an emphasis on understanding the chemical and microbiological processes of wine making.

This program will teach you to use a scientific approach to assess wine qualities, evaluate the stability of wine, understand the mechanisms of sensory perception, and apply fundamental principles of analytical chemistry. It also covers the factors behind growing quality grapes. After the completion of five college courses, 18.5 credits, you'll earn your college certificate.

Link:
https://cpe.ucdavis.edu/certificate-program/winemaking-certificate-program

Course Level: Advanced

Course Length: 18 Months

Cost: $8810 USD

Washington State University Certificate Programs

Washington State University offers two online non-credit professional certificate programs: a Viticulture Certificate and an Enology Certificate. These are designed for those interested in the grape and wine industry and are taught by WSU faculty and business leaders from the Washington wine industry.

The courses are taught over a year and a half. And three weekend camps provide students with hands-on experience where they will directly grapevines, crush grapes, and conduct laboratory analyses. The viticulture certificate dives into all aspects of growing grapes. It consists of 11 courses discussing everything from soil and nutrient management to disease control. The enology certificate covers all aspects of the winemaking process, from winery equipment and sanitation to compliance and labeling.

Link: http://wine.wsu.edu/education/certificate/

Course Level: Advanced

Course Length: 20 Months

Cost: $5,995 USD

CONCLUSION

As you learn more about wine by attending tastings at stores or vineyards, additional online education can help improve your knowledge and appreciation of wine. In an increasingly connected world, e-learning can bring experts to your living room and goes beyond what can be learned locally. A variety of classes are available to choose from at all price points and levels of commitment. Some are simply for personal enjoyment, while others prepare you for work in the wine industry.

CHAPTER 7: SELECTING, STORING, AND SERVING WINE

"Wine is a living liquid containing no preservatives. Its life cycle comprises youth, maturity, old age, and death. When not treated with reasonable respect it will sicken and die."

- Julia Child

At first, purchasing a bottle of wine doesn't seem difficult. It seems as easy as entering a store, choosing a bottle, and checking out. But when you actually walk into a wine retailer and see the aisles filled with hundreds of choices, it suddenly seems much more difficult.

Because there are so many different kinds of wines and just as many personal preferences, finding the right one can seem impossible. By properly preparing yourself before you go to the store, you can find the bottle of wine.

SELECTING THE RIGHT WINE

Before setting off to buy a bottle of wine, you need to do a few things. You need to properly prepare yourself for the experience. Knowing what you want before you arrive at the liquor store helps immensely. And understanding the ways that wines are labeled is equally important. These two things will make wine shopping easier. You might even find that shopping for wine can be enjoyable. Wine shopping can be an experience unto itself, just as drinking the wine can be.

The first question to consider is why am I buying a bottle of wine? Am I celebrating a special occasion, like a wedding or college graduation? Or am I just looking to entertain some friends? Do I want something to pair with the dinner I am cooking? Or am I looking for a sweet after dinner treat? If I am hosting a party, is it a formal even or an information get-together? The answers to these questions might point you in the right direction.

Each event may dictate that a different wine be chosen. For a cocktail party, you might choose a softer, lighter style of wine. Maybe a Chenin Blanc or Riesling? For a dinner party, it might be more appropriate to choose a drier, white wine that can stimulate the appetite. Maybe a French Muscadet or a California Chardonnay? You might even want to serve a sweet sparkling dessert wine afterwards. Could I suggest Moscato d'Asti or an Asti Spumante? As for a wedding a more middle of the road sparkling wine might be in order. How about a Sparkling Gewürztraminer?

Once you know the purpose for purchasing the wine, you want to consider the price. How much are you willing to spend? Wine prices range from a few dollars a bottle to tens of thousands of dollars. You can go with an inexpensive bag or judge or for moderately priced table wines, depending upon the occasion.

Once you know what kind of wine you want, or at least the characteristics you're looking for, and the price you can afford, you can consider the retailer. Depending upon the laws of your particular state, you have a variety of options. These include grocery stores, big box retailers, liquor stores, specialty wine sellers, and even auctions. And in most states, you can have wine delivered to your door, so the Internet is an option.

The selection and range varies depending upon the type of retailer you choose. Wine stores will typically have a larger selection and feature better wines. The most expensive wines sell at auction. Liquor stores often balance selection and prices. Grocery stores and big box offer more affordable options, but have less to choose from.

No matter where you shop, each of these options provides

you with a chance to learn more about and discover new wines. But you have to consider that the knowledge you can rely on at a generic store is likely considerably lower than it would be if you went to a retailer that specializes in wine or spirits.

As a beginner, you're not likely to purchase wine at auction. Wine here is often purchased as an investment, and therefore needs to be authenticated. This is best left to the experts. If you choose to shop online, you should be careful. Some wines don't ship well and if you're looking at a more expensive brand, there is a small chance that the wine could be a fake imitation of the real thing. Small and unknown sites have been known to prey on unsuspecting individuals.

If you live near a winery, you can always go right to the source. But this means being limited to the selection that they have and many people don't live in one of the major wine producing territories. For most beginners, I'd suggest shopping at a dedicated liquor or wine store. There you will likely find knowledgeable staff that can help.

If you can, you should bring a wine guide or checklist. You should also practice reading wine labels beforehand. I've included a sample label in this book that shows where you can find all of the important information. The benefit here is that you will know exactly what you are getting. Even if vintage and region is not meaningful to you yet, it eventually will be. A general rule of thumb to remember is that the more specific and detailed the wine label is, the higher the quality of wine is likely to be.

The Anatomy of a Wine Label

Labels contain a lot of information. The movement around the world is trending towards clear detailed labeling. This benefits the consumer. Because the more information at the consumers disposable, the more confident he can be that he knows what he is getting. Some of the information that you can find on the wine labels are listed here.

- The name of the wine
- The type of wine
- The name of the producer
- The state or country of origin

[77]

- The total volume of wine
- The alcohol content

If you go to a wine store, it might help making choosing a wine easier. They usually arrange the wine by the country of origin or by producer. Within each section the wine may also be organized into white and red sections. You'll need to consult your list and your budget before making a choice.

If you're shopping at a liquor store, they sometimes group the wines by variety. Pay attention to how the store is arranged at it'll make it easier to find what you are looking for.

If you want a finer wine, you may have to ask for help. Sometimes a special room is reserved for the more expensive wines. On the other end of the spectrum, you may want to check to see if there is a bargain bin.

Do not be afraid to ask the retailer about the wines. This is an opportunity to discuss and learn more about wine. Even a simple question could lead to you learning more. A good retailer would be happy to answer your questions or even assist with selecting the perfect wine.

A good wine merchant will offer wines at a variety of prices. He will display a wide range of selection and will have some amount of training in wine. There should also be some indication that the wine has been properly stored.

It may even offer in-store tastings or have samples available.

Don't be afraid to try something new. Exploring the many great wines of the world can be its own journey. Take opportunities to expand your taste buds. You'll find that there are some wines that are simply undrinkable and others that may be irresistible. When I go shopping for wine, I always try to pick up two bottles, one I love and one I've never tried.

SERVING WINE

There may be an air of sophistication surrounding wine service. But for the most part that's theater. There is a traditional way to serve wine, which we will discuss in the next chapter, but when you're hosting, there's no pressure to follow the set-pattern. You can be less formal, as I am at home, or you might want enjoy serving your guests with formalities. It's entirely up to you.

Serving wine involves only three basic steps: open, pour, serve. The finer points of traditional service are really just for show. There are some details that you need to remember.

For example, you need to chill most white wines. Red wines, for the most part, should be served at room temperature. This does not mean they cannot be chilled. Some people will chill them for an hour or so before removing them from the cooler where they will then allow them to approach room temperature. But keep in mind that these are general rules. They don't apply in all cases. One exception I can think of involves Concord wine. Because concord grapes are extraordinarily sweet, they get chilled even though they are red in appearance.

Once your wine is at the proper temperature, you will remove the cork or unscrew the cap. There are a variety of tools available for this purpose. But the trust old wire corkscrew is definitely the most well-known.

After you remove the cork, you have a few different options. You can go ahead and pour the wine. Or if you prefer, decant the wine. Some people will leave it in the bottle for a moment so that it can "breathe." One purpose of decanting and the reason some people will allow the wine to breath for a moment, is because it helps remove any of the off-odors. Pouring the wine into a carafe, decanter or glass can also help the wine breathe. Decanting serves other purposes as well. It helps to removes some of the sediment in the wine.

The final step in wine service is the pour. Whether you go

straight from the bottle or from a carafe, pouring the wine
is the last step.

When pouring wine, you should use the proper glass and
fill it to the proper level. There are variations between red
and white wine glasses and even specialized glasses for
certain wines. Red wine glasses are generally rounded
with larger bowls and wider openings than white wines.
You never fill a standard wine glass up completely.
Instead, you would typically fill red wine glass about a

[81]

third of the way and white wine glasses about halfway.

We'll go over this again later, but you should know that a standard pour for either one is five ounces. That means, you should get about five glasses to a bottle. And there are actually a number of specialized wine glasses. For example, tall, slim flutes are always used when serving Champagne.

STORING WINE

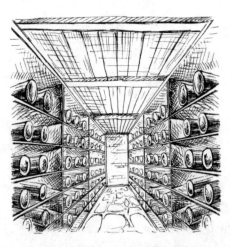

Storing wine may or may not be necessary, depending on how long you plan to keep the wine. If you buy wine and plan on serving it soon, there is no reason to invest in elaborate wine storage. You place your whites in a refrigerator and your reds on a shelf without problems. For long term storage of wine, you will need specialized storage. The type of storage you need is based on the type and quality of the wine.

Some wine will improve with age, but most will not. For wines that improve with age, the typical answer is the wine cellar. But most people don't have access to a cool, dark wine cellar, so other options for storing wine include using a cool, dark closet, storage options at a wine shop, or buying a wine cave. Collectors use climate controlled options that kept ideal temperatures and humidity levels. But for most of us that is not realistic.

When storing wine, the most important thing to is to keep the environment constant. Temperatures should always be stable. A good temperature that works for the storage of red or white wine is around 55°F, with approximately 70% humidity. Extreme temperatures or exposure to continuous light will ruin the wine.

While fine wine may last decades in a wine cellar, most red wines should be consumed within three years of the expiration date and most whites within two. After opening the wine though you must drink it pretty quickly. An opened white can be refrigerated for a few days and a red will hold for about a week.

CONCLUSION

Buying wine can be baffling if you are a newbie. Always go to the store prepared. Take a list or a wine guide. Be open to talking to the wine shop merchant or retailer about what you want. Be adventurous in your choice when you can.

At home, follow appropriate procedures for both serving and storing wine. You may prepare and serve according to tradition or adopt your own procedures. As long as it meets the demands of the wine, be free to utilize your skills and knowledge. Read up on serving etiquette and storage procedures. You are a newbie. The more you read, the more you will discover about what may become your favorite subject – wine. You may even decide to venture into the next level of this world – wine tasting.

CHAPTER 8: SELECTING WINE IN A RESTAURANT

"For at the end of the day, what matters is never the wine, it's always the moment; it's always the people."

— *Olivier Magny, Into Wine: An Invitation to Pleasure*

Ordering wine doesn't have to be difficult. You can simply order the house white or house red. Or, if you want to be specific, then you'll want to ask for a wine list. You base your decision on what is available and what you can afford. When there is a large selection of wine, things can be a bit overwhelming for the novice. If the restaurant has a large selection of wines and a variety of prices, you'll want to examine the wine list carefully. Order based upon what you've learned about wine. You definitely don't want make your choice at random.

UNDERSTANDING THE WINE LIST

Wine lists come in a variety of types and sizes. At a more casual establishment, you might see the choices scribbled on a chalkboard. Or the wine list may be a limited selection on the back of the regular menu. Even still, you can likely find a wine that you'll enjoy. Dining rooms that have limited availability make it a point to stock more popular selections. At nicer places, the wine list may come on a separate menu, mixed in or integrated with other adult beverages.

It's important to note that not all wine lists are created equal. There are good lists and bad ones. Either way, you must absorb the available information to make the most informed choice. Maybe you'll find a favorite. If not,  your decision will be guided by your knowledge of the different grapes and regions, as well as your own preferences and the preferences of those who are dining with you.

When I say a good wine list or a bad one, I am not referring to the quality of the wines, although this is certainly a factor. I'm referring to the arrangement of the selections on the list and the amount of included information. A bad list leaves out information that can be pertinent to making a good selection. Maybe it neglects to mention the price, the name of the wine, or the vintage. A good wine list, on the other hand, will provide enough information upon which to base your decision.

A well thought out wine list is sign that the establishment takes wine seriously. Your ability to understand the information allows you to make an informed decision. You should know that a good wine list will do all of the following.

- It will group the wines by color, and by place of origin or by some other means. For example, the Melting Pot has their wines arranged first by color and then by sweetness. The lighter wines in each group are listed first and as the list progresses you come to more full bodied wines.

- It will clearly provide the name of the wine and will show you where the wine came from or who made it. For the more experienced wine consumer, this can prevent you from selecting a mediocre selection.

- It will list the vintage. Quality can vary from year to year and knowing how a particular region did in any given year can be valuable information to have at your disposable. Ideally, you want to get the best wine within your price range, which brings us to the next point.

- It should also provide you with the price. I'd never order a wine where the price wasn't disclosed in advance. A key determining factor for most people is the price point.

- An above average wine list will also give provide you with a bin number. Instead of mispronouncing the name of an unfamiliar wine, you can simply give the server or sommelier a specific number.

All of the information on the wine list serves the customer. The intent of this information is to help you select the right wine to pair with your meal or make it easy for you to discover a new favorite.

ASKING FOR ASSISTANCE

If you are not sure, what to order you should always ask someone. If there is a sommelier, he can guide you towards a wine that will satisfy. It would be worth describing your preferences. Their job isn't to push a wine on you that you won't like. Instead, the sommelier is there help you find something that works for you. A good sommelier will never make you feel ignorant. On the contrary, he is there to make you feel comfortable with your selection.

If there is no sommelier, you can always ask your server. At a high end restaurant, the server is often your best friend when it comes to choosing the right wine. Not only are they often trained in the available wines, but they have often tried them. As the first line work, serving the customers, he or she often has first-hand knowledge as to which wines past customers have liked or disliked. The serve may be able to provide some guidance. Either way, you should still ask to see a wine list.

PRESENTATION

The presentation at different restaurants varies in method and formality. There are formal and informal ways of serving wine at a restaurant. If you order by the glass, the waiter will bring you the wine in a separate container, known as a carafe, to pour into the glass. When ordering by the bottle though, the formalities often kick in. The traditional way of serving the wine is for the server to bring the bottle and present it before opening. You should always read the label to be sure that the wine presented is the one you ordered. While rare, people do make mistakes.

Then, if one is present, your server will remove the cork and present it to the person who ordered the bottle. At this point, you should smell the cork and touch it. Check to see if it crumbles. If it does, it could indicate problems with the wine. You should also examine the cork to ensure that it matches the wine. The cork is offered as proof that the brand given agrees with what is written on the bottle. Unfortunately, wine fraud is becoming more common with the more expensive wines.

Assuming everything is ok, once you have "sniffed" the cork, you should nod positively to the server. He or she will then pour a sample of the wine into a glass. This is your opportunity to inspect the wine. You will look at its color. Next, you will swirl the wine to release the aroma before you taste it. And then of course you will swallow it.

If there is a problem with the wine, this is the time to notify your server. A restaurant will replace your wine if the wine is faulty, but it has no obligation to replace the wine because you do not like it.

If the wine is acceptable, you should thank your server. He will then offer to pour a glass for anyone else at the table who would like one. This is the formal way of presenting wine. At more casual establishments, which lack expensive selections, you may find that the server may simply drop the bottle off at the table. If you ordered a sparkling wine, the server should leave an ice bucket on the table to keep your bottle cold.

Remember, white wine glasses should be filled one-half full and red wine glasses are filled about one-third of the way. This allows you to give your reds a good swirl. And although the server will often come by and refill your glasses, it's always proper to offer to top off your dinner guests glass.

CONCLUSION

Ordering wine in a restaurant may seem difficult at first. And there might be a time that you order something you don't care for. You should, however, consider that part of your education. Hopefully, though, you'll be pleasantly surprised with your selections. You shouldn't be afraid to ask for help. When it comes to wine every glass is part of the learning experience. You need work to expand your knowledge of wine and have a basic understanding of etiquette. Learning to read and understand the arrangement of various wine lists can help you along the way. The more practice you get at ordering wine, the more comfortable you will become.

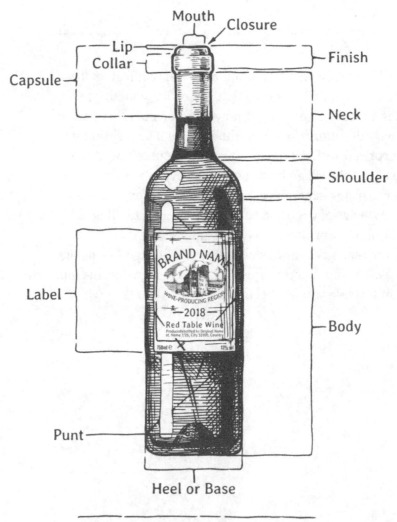

Mouth

Closure

Lip

Collar

Finish

Capsule

Neck

Shoulder

Label

Body

Punt

Heel or Base

The Anatomy of a Wine Bottle

CHAPTER 9: EUROPEAN WINE

"A bottle of wine contains more philosophy than all the books in the world."

-Louis Pasteur, French Biologist and Chemist

Europe has a rich history of winemaking. Accordingly, it is home to the top three wine producing countries in the world: France, Italy, and Spain. Visiting the stunningly exquisite vineyards with their enchanting hillsides is a dream for every wine connoisseur. There are, of course, other countries producing amazing wines, but we've chosen to focus on wines from the big three producers as they make the wines you are most likely to encounter.

That's not say you shouldn't try a port wine from the Douro Valley in Portugal or a Riesling from the Mosel wine region of Germany, but since this is a guide for beginners, we chose not to overload you with information. Once you get the basics down, you can venture of to the lessor known locales, like Istria in Croatia to discover the Malvasia Istriana, a white grape that forms a fresh, fruity wine, or Teran, which develops into a rich, earthy red. But for now, we'll spare you from having to learn that Santorini in Greece is famous for Assyrtiko or that Lavaux in Switzerland makes light, crisp whites from the Chasselas grape.

We'll begin our journey into European wine with something more approachable: the wine regions of France, Italy, and Spain.

FRANCE

France produces an incredible amount of wine, between seven and eight billion bottles. French winemaking is full of tradition, tracing its history back to the sixth century BC with many of the winemaking regions dating their history to Roman times. The concept of *terroir* is central to French winemaking, which links the style of the wines to the locations where the grapes are grown and the wine is made.

Winemaking in France is part of the nation's history and remains an important part of the culture. French wine originated with the colonization of Southern Gaul by Greek Settlers. Viticulture soon flourished. Today, France has several hundred geographically defined appellations. The country of France is the source of many grape varieties. Cabernet Sauvignon, Chardonnay, Pinot Noir and Sauvignon blanc all claim France as their motherland. Wines from Burgundy and Bordeaux often demand premium prices.

France produces all of the common styles of wine and most are meant to accompany food. Since French tradition is to serve wine with food, few of the wines were developed for drinking on their own. A wide variety of grapes are cultivated in France. Most are associated with a particular region. Cabernet Sauvignon is associated with Bordeaux and Syrah with Rhône for example.

Because French wines are almost always associated with a certain region, we'll take a closer look at the well-known wine regions of France.

CHAMPAGNE

We'll start with Champagne, because it is one of the most well-known wine producing regions, even among non-connoisseurs. The name of this region is a household name, one associated with sparkling wine. By law, only a sparkling wine made here can be called Champagne. Any other wine with bubbles is simply sparkling wine. It is a region with the beautiful rolling hillsides full of vineyards producing both white and rosé wines. The principal grapes of the region are Chardonnay, Pinot noir, and Pinot Meunier.

BORDEAUX

Bordeaux is known, informally, as the wine capital of the world. It is a large region on the Atlantic coast, the enthralling blend of history, medieval culture, and fine cuisine make Bordeaux a choice destination. This is primarily a red wine region, famous for the wines Château Lafite-Rothschild, Château Latour, Château Mouton-Rothschild, and Château Margaux. The red wines produced are usually blended from Cabernet Sauvignon and Merlot.

BURGUNDY

Burgundy is a region in eastern France where both red and white wines are equally important. Burgundy is divided into more appellations than any other French region, reflecting its terroir-consciousness. The top wines from the heartland in Côte d'Or command high prices. Although a variety of grapes are grown, the two main varieties in Burgundy are Chardonnay for white wines and Pinot noir for red ones.

THE LOIRE VALLEY

The Loire Valley spans 280 kilometers along a stretch of the Loire River in central France. It is primarily a white-wine region. Grape varieties and wine styles vary along the river, but the grapes most characteristic of this area are Chenin Blanc, Sauvignon Blanc, and Melon de Bourgogne. The area is ideal for a romantic getaway, as the area boasts some incredible castles you can visit.

THE RHÔNE VALLEY

The Rhône wine region is paradise for wine lovers. While wandering through its rugged hillside you can visit the locations where Côtes du Rhône, Côte-Rôtie, and Beaumes-de-Venise are produced. The area is divided into two sub-regions, northern and southern Rhône. In the northern sub-region you find red wines made from Syrah and white wines made from Roussanne and Viognier grapes. The southern sub-region produces an array of reds, whites, and rosé wines. You'll often find blends, the most prestigious of which is Châteauneuf-du-Pape.

SAVOY WINE REGION

The Savoy, (or Savoie) is a smaller, lesser known wine region in France that stretches from Geneva, Switzerland down to the region surrounding Chambery. The Savoy landscape is distinctly alpine, so the vineyards of Savoy are often planted on very steep slopes. The primarily produces white wines with Altesse and Roussanne grapes, but here you can also find a unique red, the Mondeuse.

I could have easily put Italy first in my list of European wine countries. But they always have that honor. Italy is the largest wine producing country in the world, with more than 1.7 million acres of cultivated vineyards. The country produces 19 percent of the world's wine. The practice of wine making in Italy goes back far, as it is home to some of the oldest wine producing regions.

Before Rome was, Etruscans and Greek settlers produced wine in Italy. The Romans perfected the craft of making wine here by developing efficient viticultural and wine making methods for large scale production and devising techniques to store the wine. It was here in Italy that barrel-making and bottling came to be.

With Greek colonization, wine-making began to thrive. During the Roman defeat of the Carthaginians, wine production exploded. Large slave-run plantations flourished to such a degree that in 92 CE, Emperor Domitian was forced to destroy a great number of vineyards to free up the land for food production. During this time, viticulture was actually banned everywhere but Italy.

Learning about Italian wine can be difficult because they use an esoteric wine labeling system, similar to the French. But that isn't the hardest part about familiarizing yourself with Italian wines. The hardest will be learning all the different grape varieties. There are more than 1,000 different grape varieties, 350 of which are officially recognized. So it's no wonder why the country has such a rich tradition with wine.

Modern wine making producers often carry traditions that go back centuries.   In many cases, they are making wine the same ways and on the same plots that their ancestors did. We are going to look at the most popular wine regions for a glimpse into those traditions. But to really know all there is to know about Italian wine, it would take a life-time of relentless study.

TUSCANY

We'll start with Tuscany, as it is arguably Italy's most famous wine growing region. The countryside of Tuscany consists of towns and cities built atop warm, sun-drenched. Lush green landscapes create incredible views. Wine aficionados flock to Tuscany for the opportunity to enjoy the finest wines in one of the worlds most enchanted places.

Tuscany can be divided into several sub-regions, with recognizable names such as Chianti, Brunello di Montalcino and Montepulciano. The region is known for its reds, but also produces dry whites and sweet wines. If I had to choose a key grape for Tuscany, without a doubt, I'd say it's Sangiovese.

PIEDMONTE

Piedmont is a northerly region famous for its red wines, like Barolo and Barbaresco. But it also produces the tannic Nebbiolo, Dolcetto, and the delicate Moscato. The region is nestled at the foot of the Alps and the Appenine mountain chain. The land is home to castles and often shrouded in mist. The Moscato d'Asti wines that the area produces are ethereally light, florally perfumed, and rather sweet.

VENETO

The largest wine making region in the Northeast part of Italy doesn't have a name that carries the prestige of Tuscany or Piedmont, but it is home some famous wines. The region produces nearly a fifth of Italy's wine.

The area produces red, white, and sparkling wines of notoriety from grapes that are seldom used elsewhere in the country. Of these Corvina is the most famous. It is typically grown along the banks of Lake Garda to make the complex and slightly sweet wines of Valpolicella and Amarone della Valpolicella. Another, Garganega is marked by aromas of peach blossom, almond, and backed golden apples. A third wine to mention is Prosecco which is used to make inexpensive and delicious sparkling wines.

PUGLIA

Puglia is located in the boot heel of Italy. Puglia is often overlooked as a wine producer, but the area is the second-largest cultivator of wine grapes in the country, behind Veneto. In the past, Puglia's reputation was marred by bulk juice production to bolster blends made elsewhere. But, now, the area's popularity is on the rice.

Puglia may be best known for its Primitivo and Negroamaro wines. Primitivo is actually the same grape that is known in California as Zinfandel. Here, it produces incredibly rich wines with spicy, dark berry tones. Negroamaro gives us savory, well-mannered reds that offer berry flavors and earthy notes. Though lessor known, the region also has produces white wines made from Falanghina, Verdeca and Muscat.

SPAIN

Spain has planted nearly three million acres of land, making it the largest wine cultivator, even if it is only the third largest producer of wine. This could be due to soil conditions, which often produce low yields. But the country produces a variety of wine. Spain has an abundance of native grape varieties, even though eighty percent of the country's wine production comes from just 20 grapes.

Like most of Europe, Spain can trace its wine history back thousands of years. Spanish wine was traded throughout the Roman Empire. Archaeologists believe that grape cultivation goes back more than five thousand years, to at least 3000 BCE, long before the Phoenicians founded the trading post of Cádiz.

The red wines the country is known for include both red and whites. The Tempranillo, Garnacha, and Monastrell are all red. Whereas, the Albariño, Verdejo, and Macabeo are white. Spain is home to a number of popular wine regions, including the Rioja, Ribera del Duero, and Jerez de la Frontera where Sherry is made.

LA RIOJA

In Spain, Rioja is synonymous with wine. The region is settled in the foothills of the Pyrenees Mountains in North-Central Spain, near the Ebro River. It is the home to more than five hundred wineries of all sizes, from family-owned operations to major industrial wineries. Together, the winemakers of Rioja pump out millions of bottles of wine each single year.

Rioja wines can vary in style, but region is best known for its Tempranillo wines. These wines are aged sold at just the right drinking age to be properly enjoyed. Sometimes they are blended with Maturana Tinta, Garnacha, or some other grape. This combines sweet flavors with rich, sour ones, producing some of the world's most unique wines.

Although some joven (young) wines are released, most Rioja wines spend some time aging. Crianzas spend two years aging, one in a barrel and another in the bottle. Reservas spend one a barrel and at least two in the bottle. The finest wines of the region, Gran Reservas, take five years to perfect. They spend their first two years aging in an oak barrel before aging another three in the bottle. The end result is an elegant wine worthy of the name Rioja.

CATALONIA

Catalonia is one of the oldest wine producing regions in Spain and can be divided into as many as 11 areas. It has a long history that is now being celebrated by new winemakers who dream of merging the old wine traditions with the new practices to produce excellent wines.

The Catalonia wine region north and to the south of Barcelona for about 90 miles along the coastline and almost as many miles inland. This vast region is famous for its Cava, a sparkling wine. The grapes of Catalonia are the red grapes Garnacha and Carignan. But, the area grows others for blending.

RIBERA DEL DUERO

The Ribera del Duero wine region is located on a plateau in the southern plains of Burgos province and, as the name implies, it stretches along the Duero River. This is an area with low to moderate rainfall and long dry summers. The area is home to a few castles and a number of interesting religious sites, including the Church of Santa Maria and the Church of San Juan.

In the Ribera grapes grown are almost exclusively red – only one white grape, the Albillo, is grown here. Most of the wine produced in this region is Tempranillo with very little mixing or blending. The ageing requirements are similar to those of Rioja.

JEREZ DE LA FRONTERA

Jerez is gets its name from the largest city in the area, Jerez de la Frontera. The city sits on one of many hills that fill the open landscape. Jerez has a reputation in the wine world. It is the fountainhead of Sherry wines. True Sherry comes from the vineyards surrounding Jerez de la Frontera and the nearby coastal towns of Puerto de Santa Maria and Sanlúcar de Barrameda. These three cites form what is known as the Sherry Triangle.

The regions soil and climate are key. The soil is albariza, or a white marl composed of clay, calcium, and marine fossils. This type of soil reflects sunlight well. In other words it has a high albedo. The coastal winds moderate temperatures while the area still receives significant sunlight. Actually, the area's 300 days of sunlight is vital to achieving optimal ripeness for the grapes. The principle grapes are the Palomino Fino and Pedro Ximenez.

CONCLUSION

Europe offers a rich history and variety of wine. It can take years before you scratch the surface of understanding all the variations and styles of wine produced there. But, the enjoyment of wine is tied to the culture, customs, and environment of the nation producing it. This chapter only served to highlight some of most popular European wines. There are so many more to explore.

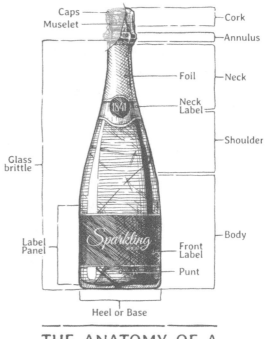

THE ANATOMY OF A
CHAMPAGNE BOTTLE

CHAPTER 10: AMERICAN WINE

"Wine makes daily living easier, less hurried, with fewer tensions and more tolerance."

--Benjamin Franklin, American Scientist and Inventor

Wine has been produced in the United States since at least the 1500s. Today wine production takes place in all fifty states, with California producing an incredible 89 percent of all US wine. The North American continent is home to several native species of grape including *Vitis labrusca*, *Vitis riparia*, *Vitis rotundifolia,* and *Vitis vulpine*. As a result, you will often find wines here that you won't find anywhere else. Still, the wine –making industry is still almost entirely based on the cultivation of the European *Vitis vinifera*.

There are more than a million acres of land dedicated to the vine, which makes the United States the fourth-largest wine producer, after Italy, Spain, and France. But The United States is not the only place to discover new wine in the Americas. You'll also find quality offerings in Argentina, Canada, and Chili. We'll look at those first, before diving into wines from the States.

ARGENTINA

Argentina is the fifth largest wine producer in the world. Argentinean wine, as with some aspects of the cuisine, has its roots in Spain, during the Spanish colonization of the Americas, vine cuttings were brought to Santiago del Estero in 1557. With time, cultivation of the grape spread to neighboring regions. Historically, Argentine winemakers were more concerned with quantity than quality, but that has changed.

The nation's most important wine regions are located in the provinces of Mendoza, San Juan, and La Rioja. The high altitude and low humidity of the wine producing regions mean that Argentine vineyards rarely face the insect, fungi, and disease problems that vineyards in other countries face. The country grows a large variety of grapes, which reflects the country's many immigrant groups. The French brought Malbec and the Italians brought Bonarda (which may be the same as Charbono in California).

We'll know look at the important wine regions of Argentina individually and highlight their unique features and differences.

MENDOZA

Mendoza is the leading producer of wine in Argentina. This one region has about half the growing area of the entire United States. The vineyards here are planted at altitudes 2,000-3,600 feet above sea level. The soil is sandy and alluvia and the area has a continental climate with four distinct seasons.

Historically, the region was dominated by high yield, pink-skinned varieties of grapes, such as the Cereza and Criolla Grande, but Malbec has become popular more recently. The high altitudes of vineyards in the Tupungato area produce excellent Chardonnay, whereas the cooler climate and lower salinity of the soils in the Maipú area make for excellent Cabernet Sauvignon.

SAN JUAN

Following Mendoza, the San Juan region produces the second largest quantity of wine in Argentina. Here the climate is considerably hotter and drier with rainfall averaging six inches a year and summer temperatures regularly exceeding a hundred degrees Fahrenheit. The area produces premium red varietals from Syrah and Banarda. It has long been producing sherry-style wines, brandies, and vermouth. Cereza is grown for blending, grape juice concentrate, and raisons.

LA RIOJA

In La Rioja, you'll find wine museums, emblematic wineries, breathtaking landscapes, and ancient monuments. This area can be called the Tuscany of

Argentina. The flagship grape of the region is the noble Tempranillo, used to create delicious reds and often blended with regional grapes such as Mazuelo, Garnacha Tinta, and Graciano. The main white grape to be found here is called Garnacha Blanca, which creates rich dry wines.

CANADA

Canadian wine is produced primarily in the provinces of Ontario and British Columbia. It is perhaps most famous for its popular ice wine, but also produces standard wines. Canadian wine has been around for more than 200 years. Early settlers tried to cultivate *Vitis vinifera* grapes, but had only limited success. So instead they focused on producing wine from native species of *Vitis labrusca* and *Vitis riparia*. These particular wines have a peculiar taste that can be described as "foxy". Today, using new techniques Canada is producing *Vitis vinifera* wines with much success.

ONTARIO

The Niagara Peninsula and the Lake Erie North Shore are two of the better known wine growing regions of Ontario.

The Niagara Peninsula is the largest Viticultural Area in Canada, accounting for three quarters of its wine. The amount of sun it receives is comparable to the

Languedoc-Rousillon in France. The temperate climates can produce fruit with more complexity and intense flavors than warmer climates.

The Lake Erie North Shore covers about 500 acres along the bow-shaped shoreline of Lake Erie between Amherstburg and Leamington. The loose gravely soil, laying atop Trenton Limestone is complemented by the moderating effect of Lake Erie, allowing the area to produce some of Canada's finest wines.

Ontario is known for its incredible ice wines, but it also produces Chardonnay, Riseling, Pinot noir, and Cabernet Franc. The ice wine for which Canada is known is a type of dessert wine made from grapes that are allowed to freeze on the vine. The sugars do not freeze, but water does, allowing for a more concentrated juice to develop.

BRITISH COLUMBIA

The wines of the rolling hills of the Okanagan Valley in British Columbia are worth the five hour drive from Vancouver. The area produces both crisp whites and bold reds. With varietals such as pinot noir, pinot gris, pinot blanc, and chardonnay, it's easy to say there is something for everyone. Some of the best wineries in the Okanagan valley can be found around the historic town of Oliver, in an area called the Golden Mile (actually more like 12 miles). There, the climate fosters a longer, warmer growing season. Owing to the gravel, clay and sandy soils, the Golden Mile is suited for varietals like merlot, gewürztraminer, and cabernet sauvignon.

THE UNITED STATES

Although wines from United States are considered New World wines, the country still has a long history of wine making. In the United States, California's Napa Valley and Sonoma remain the top wine producing. But, there are plenty of other wine regions with growing influence. America is producing world-class wines, is the host of much wine tourism and many wine festivals. Although this could be a book unto itself, I'm just going to highlight the most important regions.

CALIFORNIA, THE LEADER

California is home to more than four thousand wineries. Within California, Napa Valley and Sonoma are still the templates that the other areas are trying to follow. Napa is known for its world-class Chardonnay, Merlot and Cabernet Sauvignon. Sonoma, in turn, is known for its Pinot Noir and Cabernet Sauvignon. But it too produces an excellent Chardonnay. But they aren't the only areas of California known for wine. The Central Coast and Paso Robles are up and coming.

WASHINGTON STATE

Second only to California, Washington State boasts more than 700 wineries of its own. The state has a total of 14 different American Viticultural Areas, the most popular being Walla Walla and Columbia Valley. Since the 1960s, wine production in the state has rapidly increased, with Washington wine being exported to more than 40 countries. Popular grapes in Washington include Riesling, Chardonnay, Merlot, and Syrah.

OREGON

Like Washington, Oregon has more than 700 wineries. Oregon has a much cooler than California, making it perfect for growing Pinot Noir. But it also produces fine Rieslings, Chardonnay, and Gamay. The most well-known wine region in Oregon is Willamette Valley, which has a reputation for superior Pinot Noir. As a point of interest, Willamette Valley is located at the same latitude as France's famed Burgundy region, also known for Pinot Noir.

NEW YORK STATE

The state of New York has more than 400 wineries and is host to two wine regions that attract the attention of wine aficionados. These regions are the Finger Lakes region and the North Fork. The Finger Lakes region is arguably the premier winemaking center on the East Coast. There you can see the vineyard of Dr. Konstantin Frank, who is credited with introducing fantastic grapes to the region, like Riesling and Gewürztraminer.

The other famous New your region, the North Fork region is located in Long Island. There you will find classic Bordeaux blends and an excellent Cabernet Franc. Other wine regions in the state include the Lake Erie AVA and the Hudson River Region.

MISSOURI, THE UNIQUE ONE

Missouri is perhaps most famous for producing wine in the corridor known as the Missouri Rhineland. This winegrowing region was founded by German immigrants in the early to mid-nineteenth century. By the 1880s, Missouri was the country's top wine-growing region. It was the Napa Valley of its day.

Today the state benefits from Missouri's long summers and thin rocky Ozark soil. Missouri is even known as the cave state for its many underground caverns. There, wineries often utilize the natural cellars. Missouri's most prominent variety of wine is the state grape, the Norton. But it also produces plenty of sweet wine with native grapes, such as the Concord. Most vineyards also plant French-American hybrids, such as Vignoles and Chardonel.

VIRGINIA

Virginia has a couple hundred wineries of its own. The state has a history of winemaking that goes back to the colonial era. In the early 1800's Thomas Jefferson, considered one of the great patrons of American wine, established two vineyards in his south orchard. The state has seven American Viticultural Areas and is known having a nearly 200-day long growing season. This makes it perfect for producing Chardonnay, Merlot, Vidal blanc, and Viognier. It is one of only a few places making noteworthy wines with Petit Manseng, a rich white-wine grape from Southwest France. And more recently, Virgina has become known for stunning Petit Verdot wines.

THE OTHER GREAT LAKE STATES

A number of the states surrounding the Great Lakes produce excellent wines. Pennsylvania benefits from being situated between Lake Erie to the North and the Atlantic Ocean to the East. Similarly, in Michigan, the Lake Effect helps to moderate the climate allowing for the production of exceptionally complex wines. Grapes such as the Austrian Blaufrankisch grape thrive there. The Lake Michigan Shore region is a scenic region that has been the "Napa of the Midwest." And in Ohio, the tradition of winemaking extends all the way back to the early 1820s. It became particularly famous for planting the Catawba grape.

AND FINALLY, TEXAS

Texas is home to the country's second largest wine region, Texas Hill Country. The state has been growing wine since the mid-1600s and has more than 4,500 acres of planted vineyards. The dry, sunny Texas climate is well suited for growing grapes like Tempranillo, Syrah, Albarino, and Zinfandel.

CONCLUSION

In the Americas, winemaking continues to evolve and innovate. Old favorites re-emerge and new varieties take root. Though Europe still leads, the New World is introducing the rest of the world to new possibilities. Across the United States and abroad the West is bringing new flavors and improving upon old ones. Without tradition to uphold, they forge paths that have never been forged before.

SYNOPSIS

"Wine moistens and tempers the spirit and lulls the cares of the mind to rest. It revives our joys and is oil to the dying flame of life."

– Socrates

While the world of wine can seem complicated to the newcomer, it grows on you. Wine culture has its own language and its own etiquette. Hopefully, this guide has served to introduce you to something new. But the knowledge you picked up here is only the beginning. Exploring what wine has to offer is a lifelong journey. I've introduced a number of people to wine. Many of them said they don't like wine. But far too often they discover that they just haven't found the wine they like. Wine offers such a wide range of rich flavors. I believe there is something for everybody.

But the journey is a personal one. It doesn't matter what the critics say about a particular wine. What is most important is that you discover the varieties that bring you delight. The process of learning about wine can seem foreign to many. But the language and behaviors shouldn't be a barrier. Every glass is part of the process it takes to move beyond a beginner into a seasoned connoisseur. Before you know it, you'll start sounding like an expert.

You'll be guiding people down this path that has uplifted your spirit and the spirits of so many before you.

Don't feel as though you must rush this process. As with anything new, you learn the basics first. You'll begin to accept the new terminology, even if you don't fully understand it yet. But there are always people willing to guide you. Before you know it, you'll reach the next stage, where the words develop meaning. You'll identify the subtle flavors and aromatic notes. You won't think of wine as just another beverage. Instead, you'll begin to appreciate the ways it affects your palate and the enjoyment wine brings.

When you begin on this journey one wine might as well be any other wine. But in time, you'll start to see wine from a different perspective. You learn to involve all the senses. For many, wine is a way of opening the senses. You'll discover that your taste experience brings the rest of the world closer.

APPENDIX I: WINE TERMINOLOGY

"Language is wine upon the lips."

– Virginia Woolf

Every profession, craft, and art has its own language. Wine experts have their own language to discuss the subject of wine and winemaking. This glossary of terms will help you make your way through the somewhat confusing world of wine lingo.

Admittedly, wine terminology can be confusing. But if you want to understand what you read and hear about wine, you have to understand these basic terms. The terms provided here are rather basic. But that can serve as a starting point, from which you can build.

Much of the language may be difficult to understand at the beginning, but the more you use it, the easier it will be to understand. You have to practice, practice and practice. And don't be afraid to get out there and try new wines for yourself. A nice restaurant with a decent wine list will have people on hand to help guide you.

Acidic: This refers to the taste of a wine. Acidic means that the wine tastes tart or bitter.

Aftertaste: This term refers to the residual taste left in your mouth after you swallow the wine. Depending upon the context, this could be good or bad.

Age: The amount of time the wine has spent maturing in the bottle.

Aroma: The odor, scent, or smell of the. It is the scent of the specific variety of grape used and is not to be confused with the wines "Bouquet."

Aromatic: This word is used to describe very pronounced or distinctive aromas.

Balance: As it suggests, balance refers to all of the wine components – the acids, tannins, alcohol, and fruit, and the relationship between them. Ideally, none would dominate.

Bitter: Refers to the taste and often stems from under-ripe grapes or the presence of tannin.

Black Grapes: A descriptive label applied to grapes with a reddish, bluish, or purple color that are used to make red wine.

Blend: A mixture of different types of wine grape varieties.

Bouquet: This is a more complex smell of wine aged in the bottle.

Box Wine: A cheap wine sold in boxes.

Brix: A measure of the level of sugar in the unfermented grape juice.

Complex: Refers to a wine with many levels of taste and aromas. Describes a very good wine.

Crisp: Refers to white wines with noticeable acidity. It feels clean and is the opposite of "soft."

Decanting: Refers to taking the wine and pouring it into another container before drinking it. The bottle this occurs in is sometimes called a decanter.

Dry: The opposite of sweet.

Dull: A wine without a distinct appearance, aroma or flavor.

Estate Bottled: Refers to wine that is grown, produced, and bottled by the owner of the respective vineyard.

Fermentation: The natural process which turns sugar into alcohol.

Finish: The final taste of the wine.

Firm: A wine that, because of its acidity, is structured. The opposite of flabby.

Flabby: A wine low acidity and, therefore, lacking structure and length of finish.

Fortified: A term for wines that had additional alcohol added during fermentation.

Full-Bodied: The opposite of a light wine, that is weighty in both flavor and texture.

Jug Wine: A cheap wine sold in jugs.

Length: The staying power of a wine's aftertaste.

Light-Bodied: The opposite of full-bodied wine., lacking texture, but retaining flavor.

Mouthfeel: Another word for texture.

Must: This is the juice of white grapes or the skins of black grapes before being fermented.

Nose: A term referring to the aroma or bouquet of the wine.

Oenophile: A wine connoisseur.

Proprietary Wine: Wine that has been branded for marketing reasons.

Residual Sugar: The sugar that remains in a wine after fermentation.

Robust: Describes a full-bodied wine.

Rosé: A pink semi-sweet wine.

Round: A well-balanced wine.

Sommelier: A wine steward; the individual responsible for ordering, storing and serving wine.

Sparkling Wine: The name given to any wine that bubbles or is effervescent, such as Champagne.

Short: Refers to a wine with flavor that suddenly stops before finishing.

Sweet: A distinguishing feature of wine resulting from high levels of residual sugar.

Tannin: A naturally bitter tasting substance from the skin of grapes and oak barrels.

Tart: Refers to wines with high acidity.

Taste: This is a broad term encompassing all the impressions a wine creates in your mouth.

Terroir: A French term applied to indicate the entire environmental impact of a specific plot of land or region upon the grapes and wine.

Texture: Refers to how a wine feels in your mouth; In other words, a wine's consistency.

Varietal: Refers to a specific variety of grape.

Varietal Wine: A wine made from varietal grapes, where a single varietal grape comprises the majority of the wine.

Vintage: The year the grapes were harvested.

Vintner: A person who makes wine.

Viticulture: The cultivation of grapes.

Weighty: The sensation of how the wine feels in the mouth.

If you are still unsure as to what kind of wine you should choose, there are some tried and true favorites. You should give each a try, but remember just because other people like a particular wine, it doesn't mean you will.

MOST POPULAR
Red wine varieties

MERLOT
MOST FAMOUS FOR ITS RED-FRUIT FLAVOURS (NAMELY CHERRY, PLUM AND RASPBERRY), EASY-DRINKING TANNINS AND SUPER-SOFT FINISH.

SHIRAZ
IT HAS A RANGE OF FLAVORS, FROM SMOKE, BACON, HERBS, RED AND BLACK FRUITS, WHITE AND BLACK PEPPER, TO FLORAL VIOLET NOTES.

PINOT NOIR
FLAVORS OF DARK CHERRIES, RED CURRANTS, AND BERRIES ARE COMMON, ALONG WITH NOTES OF MUSHROOM AND SOIL. YOU MIGHT TASTE HINTS OF VANILLA, SPICE, CHOCOLATE, TOBACCO, AND OAK.

CABERNET SAUVIGNON
THE MOST COMMON AROMATIC AND FLAVOR COMPONENTS FOUND IN CABERNET SAUVIGNON ARE DARK FRUITS LIKE PLUM, BLACK CHERRY, AND BLACKBERRY ALONG WITH WARM SPICE, VANILLA, LICORICE, AND BLACK PEPPER.

As you can see from the charts, the most popular red wines are Merlot, Shiraz, Pinot Noir, and Cabernet Sauvignon. Each of them has their own unique flavor and aroma. The same is true of the most popular white wine varieties. White wine favorites include Chardonnay, Riesling, Pinot Grigio, and Sauvignon Blanc. The chart below describes their unique personalities.

MOST POPULAR
white wine varieties

CHARDONNAY

CHARDONNAY IS KNOWN TO BE A RELATIVELY DRY, MEDIUM-BODIED WHITE WINE EMANATING FRESH, CRISP NOTES OF PEAR, GUAVA, LEMON-PEEL AND APPLE.

RIESLING

TYPICALLY CHARACTERISED BY LIGHT BODY AND LOW ALCOHOL LEVELS, RIESLING IS COMMONLY APPRECIATED FOR ITS NATURAL CRISP ACIDITY AND PROFOUND PERFUME, WHICH REMAIN PRESENT AT ANY LEVEL OF RIPENESS.

PINOT GRIGIO

THE PRIMARY FRUIT FLAVORS IN PINOT GRIGIO ARE LIME, LEMON, PEAR, WHITE NECTARINE AND APPLE. DEPENDING ON WHERE THE GRAPES ARE GROWN, PINOT GRIGIO CAN TAKE ON FAINT HONEYED NOTES

SAUVIGNON BLANC

HE PRIMARY FRUIT FLAVORS OF SAUVIGNON BLANC ARE LIME, GREEN APPLE, PASSION FRUIT AND WHITE PEACH. DEPENDING ON HOW RIPE THE GRAPES ARE WHEN THE WINE IS MADE, THE FLAVOR WILL RANGE FROM ZESTY LIME TO FLOWERY PEACH.

While, I always encourage you to find what works for you, I provided these descriptions to help point you in the right direction. These descriptions, along with an understanding of which wines are sweeter and drier, are a good starting point. These eight wines are what I would call the big eight. That is they are the eight wines that you should definitely know.

Furthermore, if you are looking for a particularly good example, you should consider selecting a wine from a region known for growing that particular variety. The chart that follows is a guide to popular wine varieties and their best growing regions.

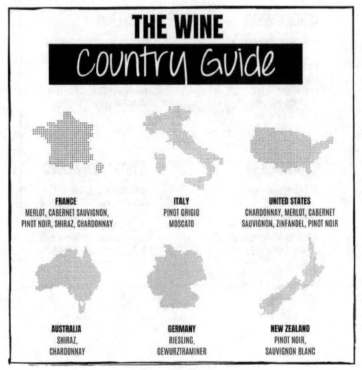

THE WINE
country Guide

FRANCE
MERLOT, CABERNET SAUVIGNON,
PINOT NOIR, SHIRAZ, CHARDONNAY

ITALY
PINOT GRIGIO
MOSCATO

UNITED STATES
CHARDONNAY, MERLOT, CABERNET
SAUVIGNON, ZINFANDEL, PINOT NOIR

AUSTRALIA
SHIRAZ,
CHARDONNAY

GERMANY
RIESLING,
GEWURZTRAMINER

NEW ZEALAND
PINOT NOIR,
SAUVIGNON BLANC

ACKNOWLEDGEMENTS

Without the help of my editor, Wes Upchurch, this book could not have been written. His assistance in writing it was invaluable. And his humility can't be quantified. It is my opinion that he should have received credit as coauthor, but he insisted that we publish this guide in my name alone. Still, I have to recognize that his wine experiences, research, and writing contributed to the completion of this book.

The blessings afforded to me that allowed me to travel the world, sample the finest wines, and dive deep into the cultures that went into them all contributed to the particular selections and recommendations that I made. I know there are a lot of wines and places that went unmentioned, but in this life we are all on our own journeys, each with our own unique experiences. I encourage you to explore wine, and the world as a whole, much deeper.

Before I go, I also wanted to thank my sister, Jessica Arnold, for making this book possible. You've been a rock when I needed one and a better friend than anyone could ever ask for.

ABOUT THE AUTHOR

Jason Murray Arnold is an art
and wine connoisseur. He's
also a professional accountant
working for large national
companies. This has afforded
him the opportunity to travel
the world in search of the
finest wines. His knowledge
goes beyond knowing how to
taste wine or simply having a deep appreciation. For
example, he has the ability to assess a young wine and
know its aging potential.

Jason is available to educate people at wine tastings, assist
collectors with the purchase of quality selections and
vintages, and to estimate the value of wine collections.
Jason has made numerous five figure acquisitions of wine
and is quite knowledgeable about all aspects of the wine
business.